BASEBALL'S WORLD SERIES

PERCY LEED

LERNER PUBLICATIONS ◆ MINNEAPOLIS

Lerner Publications Company
An imprint of Lerner Publishing Group, Inc.
241 First Avenue North
Minneapolis, MN 55401 USA

For reading levels and more information, look up this title at www.lernerbooks.com.

Main body text set in Mikado.
Typeface provided by HVD Fonts.

Photo Editor: Lucien Brinkley
Lerner team: Martha Kranes, Sue Marquis

Library of Congress Cataloging-in-Publication Data

Names: Leed, Percy, 1968– author.
Title: Baseball's World Series / Percy Leed.
Other titles: World Series
Description: Minneapolis, MN : Lerner Publications, [2025] | Series: Lerner sports rookie. Championship games | Includes bibliographical references and index. | Audience: Ages 5–8 years | Audience: Grades K–1 | Summary: "Impossible odds, thrilling comebacks, and big home runs all make the World Series exciting. Young readers will enjoy learning more about baseball's biggest game from its greatest moments to its best players and more"— Provided by publisher.
Identifiers: LCCN 2024012935 (print) | LCCN 2024012936 (ebook) | ISBN 9798765648056 (lib. bdg.) | ISBN 9798765661482 (pbk.) | ISBN 9798765653791 (epub)
Subjects: LCSH: World Series (Baseball)—Juvenile literature. | American League Championship Series (Baseball)—Juvenile literature. | National League Championship Series (Baseball)—Juvenile literature. | Baseball—United States—History—Juvenile literature.
Classification: LCC GV878.4 .L44 2025 (print) | LCC GV878.4 (ebook) | DDC 796.357/6409—dc23/eng/20240531

LC record available at https://lccn.loc.gov/2024012935
LC ebook record available at https://lccn.loc.gov/2024012936

Manufactured in the United States of America
1-1010914-53366-6/14/2024

TABLE OF CONTENTS

CHAPTER 1
THE WORLD SERIES

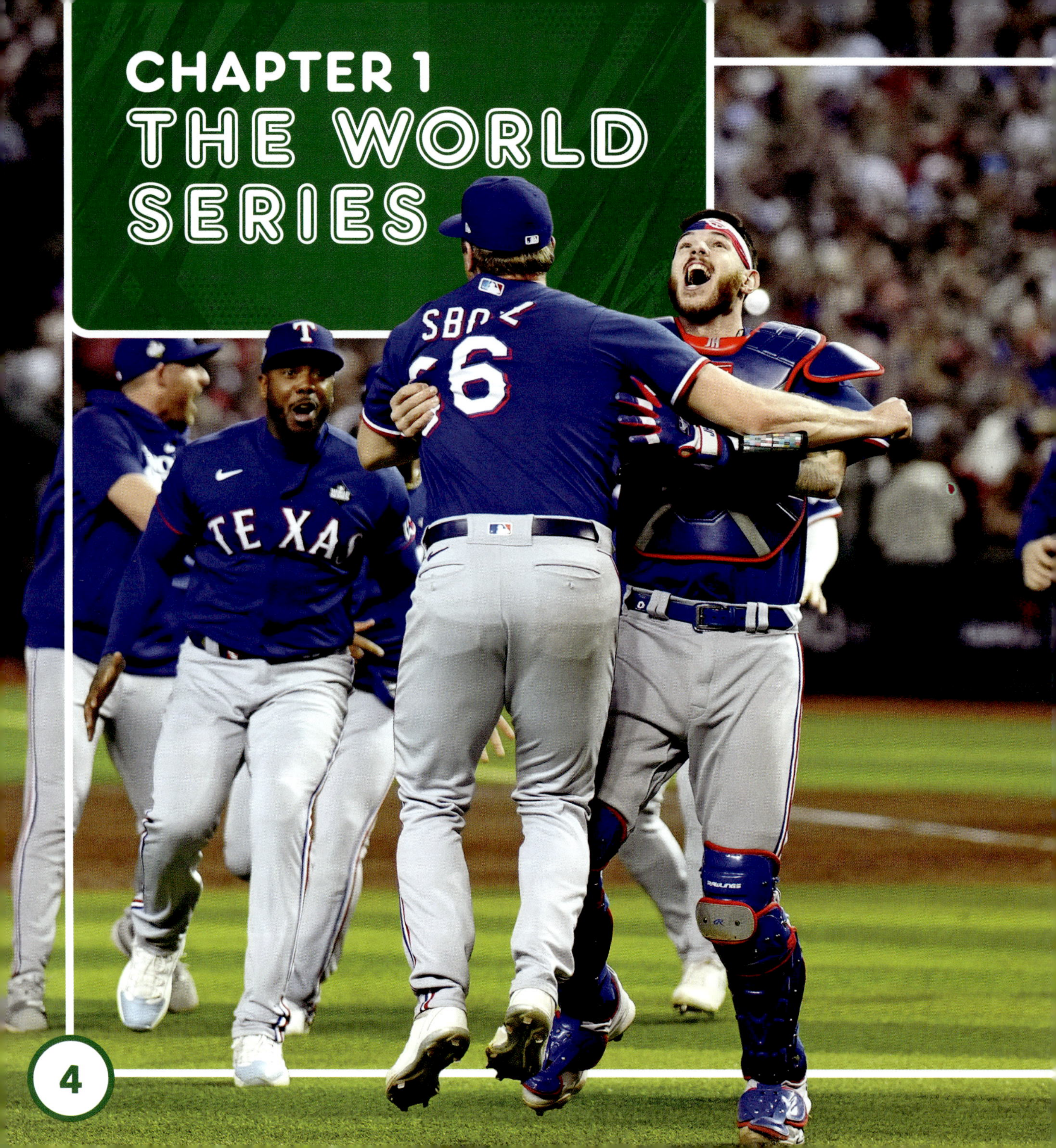

The Texas Rangers played against the Arizona Diamondbacks in the 2023 World Series. Texas won the series!

1903 World Series

The World Series started in 1903. Winners from the National League and American League play each other.

The team that wins becomes the World Series winner.

2023 World Series winners

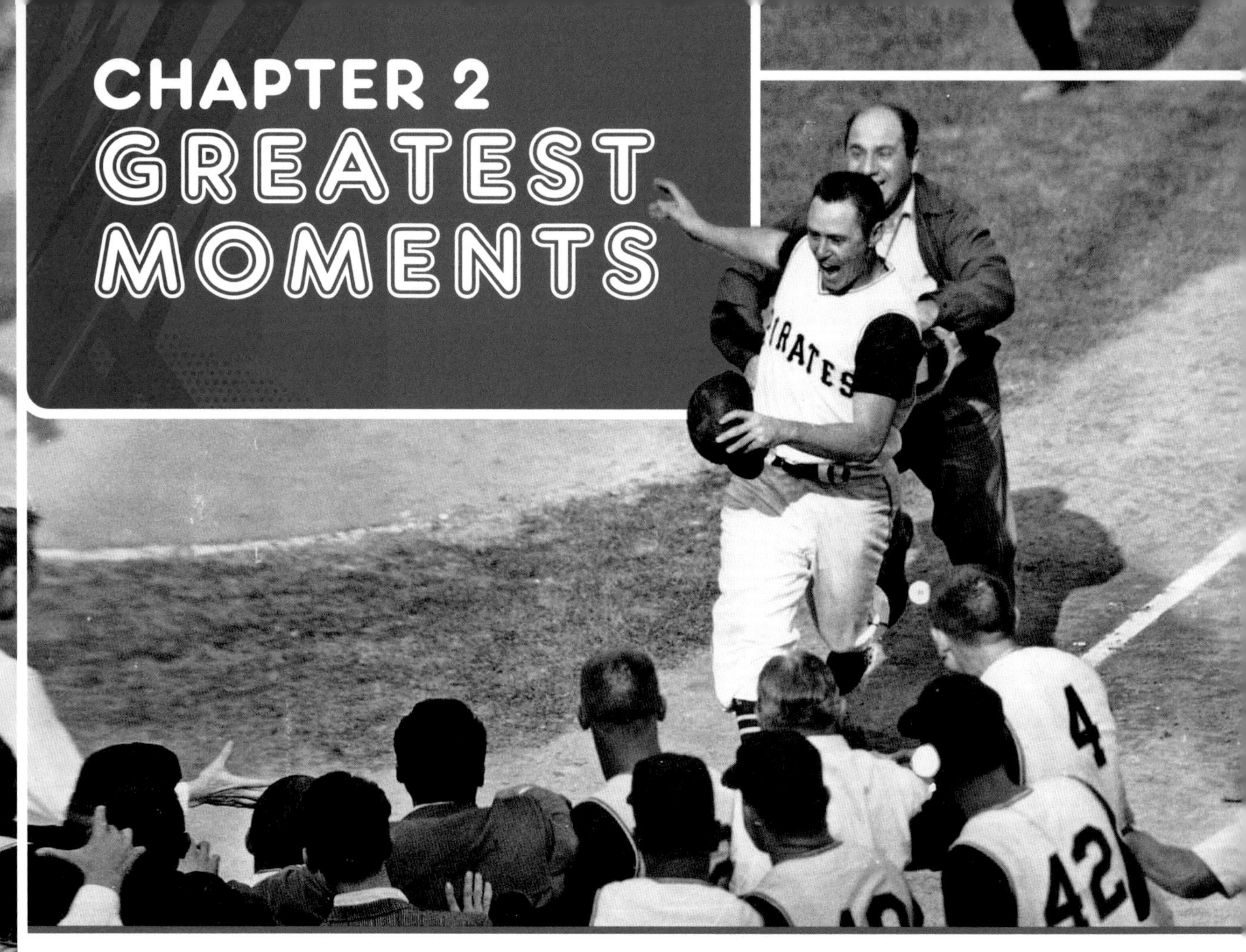

CHAPTER 2 GREATEST MOMENTS

Many people thought the Pittsburgh Pirates would lose the 1960 World Series. But in Game 7 they pulled ahead of the New York Yankees.

The Pirates hit a home run in the last inning and won.

GIBSO
23

The Los Angeles Dodgers were down 4–3 in Game 1 of the 1988 World Series. The Dodgers' best hitter, Kirk Gibson, had a hurt leg. Gibson went to bat and hit a home run. The Dodgers won!

The St. Louis Cardinals were down 7–5 in Game 6 of the 2011 World Series. They caught up to the Texas Rangers and went into extra innings.

In the 11th inning, the Cardinals scored and won.

CHAPTER 3
BEST PLAYERS

No MLB player has more World Series wins than Yogi Berra. He won 10 of them!

Reggie Jackson hit many home runs. He won the World Series five times and was named series MVP twice.

Madison Bumgarner is one of the best pitchers ever. He's played in 36 World Series innings. He only ever let one run through.

Pablo Sandoval was the fourth person in World Series history to hit three home runs in a game. He's won three World Series.

CHAPTER 4
BATTER UP

Fans pack the seats during every World Series game. The smell of hot dogs and popcorn fills the air.

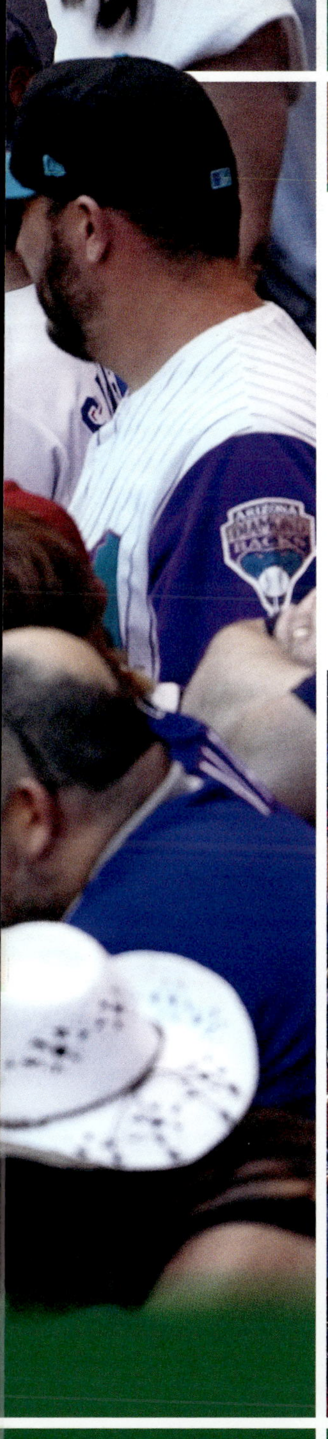

The crowd roars as the players run onto the field.

The game begins when the first batter steps up to the plate. He gets ready for the pitch. Swing! It's time to play ball.

WORLD SERIES CHAMPS

Here are recent World Series champs!

2023 Texas Rangers

2022 Houston Astros

2021 Atlanta Braves

2020 Los Angeles Dodgers

2019 Washington Nationals

2018 Boston Red Sox

2017 Houston Astros

2016 Chicago Cubs

2015 Kansas City Royals

2014 San Francisco Giants

FUN FACTS

The New York Yankees have won the most World Series at 27.

Mickey Mantle holds the record for most home runs at the World Series with 18.

The longest-ever World Series game was 18 innings and lasted seven hours and 20 minutes.

GLOSSARY

inning: a turn at bat for each team

MVP: short for *most valuable player*

run: when a player makes it around all the bases and returns to home plate to score

series: best-of-seven games

LEARN MORE

Downs, Kieran. *Baseball.* Minneapolis: Bellwether Media, 2024.

Leed, Percy. *Baseball: A First Look*. Minneapolis: Lerner Publications, 2023.

Troupe, Thomas Kingsley. *Baseball.* Minneapolis: Kaleidoscope, 2022.

INDEX

PHOTO ACKNOWLEDGMENTS

Image credits: Daniel Shirey/Stringer/Getty Images, pp. 4–5; Mark Rucker/Transcendental Graphics/Getty Images, p. 6; Caitlin O'Hara/MLB Photos via Getty Images, p. 7; AP Photo/Harry Harris, pp. 8–9; Focus on Sport/Getty Images, p. 10; AP Photo/Jeff Roberson, p. 12; AP Photo/Eric Gay, p. 13; Bettmann/Getty Images, pp. 14–15; AP Photo/Peter Southwick, p. 15; Rob Tringali/MLB Photos via Getty Images, p. 16; Brad Mangin/MLB via Getty Images, p. 17; AP Photo/Ross D. Franklin, p. 18; Chris Coduto/MLB Photos via Getty Images, p. 19; Christian Petersen/Getty Images, p. 21. Design element: Winner Creative/Shutterstock.
Cover: Kyodo via AP Images.